WASPS & BEES

Written by Graham Meadows & Claire Vial

CONTENTS

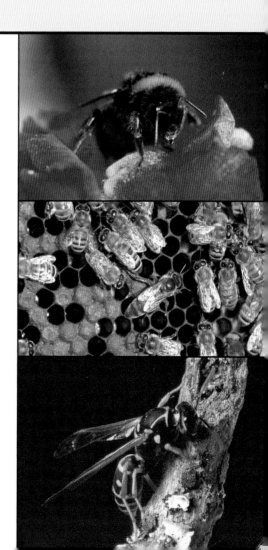

Dominie Press, Inc.

Bumblebee ▲

Honeybee ▶

2

ABOUT WASPS AND BEES

Wasps and bees are insects that are found almost everywhere in the world. They are most common in **tropical** and subtropical areas. There are about 100,000 known **species** of wasps and bees. Most wasps and bees are **solitary**. The members of a few species live together in colonies.

Many wasps and bees are yellow, orange, or black in color. Some are metallic green or blue. Others are yellow or orange with black stripes.

They have three pairs of legs and a pair of **antennae**. Their bodies have three parts: the head, the thorax, and the abdomen.

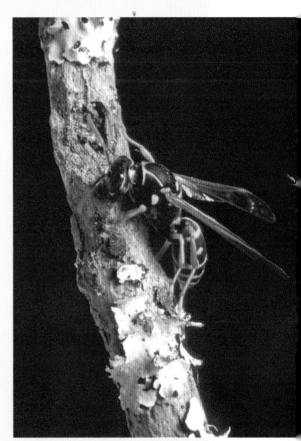

▲ **Chinese Paper Wasp**

Wasps and bees belong to a group of insects that also includes ants and sawflies.

WHAT WASPS LOOK LIKE

Most wasps have a few body hairs and what looks like a thin "wasp waist." The majority of wasp species do not sting. Wasps that sting, such as the German wasp, have a stinger that is not barbed, which means they can sting more than once. They sting their **prey** and feed it to their young. They also sting to protect themselves.

Wasps that do not sting, such as the ichneumon wasp, do not have a stinger. Instead, they have a special egg-laying tube. Some species of wasps use this tube to lay their eggs in the young of other insects and spiders. Others use their egg-laying tube to deposit their eggs in plants.

◀ **Ichneumon Wasp**

Adult wasps feed mainly on nectar from flowers.

▲ **German Wasp**

Honeybees ▲

WHAT BEES LOOK LIKE

Bees have a thick waist and a thick coat of body hair. They have pouches, or baskets, on their legs. They use their pouches to carry **pollen**.

▲ **Bumblebee Collecting Nectar from a Flower**

All bees have a stinger that is barbed. When a bee stings, the stinger is pulled out of the bee, and the bee dies. This means bees can only sting once. Bees only sting to protect themselves.

Many bees build nests made of wax. Some bees build their nests in holes or cracks in the ground, or in trees.

Adult bees collect, store, and feed on nectar and pollen from flowers.

WASPS THAT STING

Most wasps that sting are solitary. For example, a female potter wasp builds a mud nest made of several cells. She collects food, such as insects and spiders, which she **paralyzes** with her stinger. She places some of this food in each cell. She then lays an egg in each cell and seals it. Then she flies away.

When the wasp eggs hatch, each **larva** eats the food in its cell. Inside the cell, the larva changes into a pupa. The pupa changes into an adult, and the adult chews its way out of the nest.

▲ **Opened Mud Nest of a Mason Wasp**

▲ **Potter Wasp**

Chinese Paper Wasps on a Nest ▲

A few wasps that sting live in colonies. They work together to raise young wasps and collect food. For example, a female Chinese paper wasp builds a nest from chewed wood. The nest contains several cells.

She lays an egg in each cell. Each egg hatches into a larva. As each larva grows, she feeds it dead insects that she has stung. When each larva is fully grown, it changes into a pupa. The pupa changes into an adult wasp, which leaves the cell.

▲ **Female Chinese Paper Wasp Starting to Build a Nest**

The new adults help to build more cells in the nest, hunt for food, and feed new larvae. In this way, the colony grows larger.

WASPS THAT DO NOT STING

Wasps that do not sting are solitary. They do not build nests. Most of them are **parasites**. They lay their eggs in, or on, the young of other insects and spiders. The young insect or spider is called a **host**. The eggs hatch into larvae, which feed on the host, and the host dies.

Some female ichneumon wasps use their long egg-laying tube to drill through plant stems. They lay eggs on grubs inside the stems.

Ichneumon Wasp Laying Eggs ▼

▲ **Eggs of Parasitic Wasp on Caterpillar**

◄ **Grub Inside Plant Stem**

13

**Ichneumon Wasp ▶
Laying Eggs in a
Butterfly Chrysalis**

Cuckoo wasps lay their eggs in the nests of other wasps. When the young hatch out, they eat the other wasps' eggs or larvae. Then they eat any food that is in the nest.

Ichneumon wasps lay their eggs in the larvae of other insects. They insert the eggs, using a long egg-laying tube. When the eggs hatch, the young feed on the body of the host.

▼ **Cuckoo Wasp about to Lay Eggs**

SOLITARY BEES

Most bees are solitary. One example is the leafcutter bee. A female leafcutter bee finds a hole in a plant stem or tree branch. She chews out the hole to make it deeper, forming a **burrow**. Then she lines the burrow with small pieces of leaves, to make a cell. She fills the cell with pollen and nectar, and lays an egg. She then seals the cell with another piece of a leaf.

After filling the burrow with four to ten cells, she flies away. When each larva is fully grown, it changes into a pupa. The pupa changes into an adult bee and chews its way out of the cell.

A leafcutter bee can snip off a leaf in less than a minute, using its sharp mouthparts.

▲ **Leafcutter Bee Carrying a Piece of a Leaf**

Honeybees in a Beehive ▲

BEES THAT LIVE IN COLONIES

Some bees live in colonies. One example is the honeybee. Honeybees form a colony in which there are three types of members: the queen, the workers, and the drones.

Queen
The queen is a large female who starts the nest and lays eggs.

Workers
Workers are smaller females who look after the nest, take care of the young, and gather nectar and pollen for food.

Drones
Drones are males that **mate** with new queens. They do not work.

Queen   **Worker Bee**   **Male Drone**

THE LIFE CYCLE OF A HONEYBEE

A new honeybee colony starts after a new queen and her workers come together and form a **swarm**.

The swarm finds a suitable place to build a nest. The workers build the cells in the nest, and the queen lays eggs in the cells. A queen can lay up to 1,500 eggs a day. Most of the eggs will produce workers. Some eggs will produce drones. A few eggs will produce queens.

◀ **Honeybee Collecting Pollen**

The Bee's Life Cycle

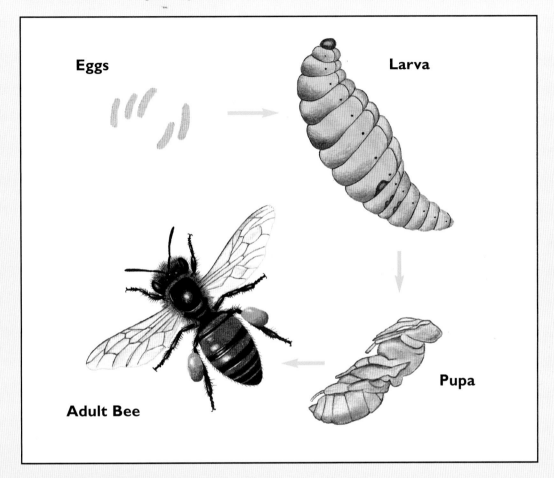

There are four stages in the bee's **life cycle**: egg, larva, pupa, and adult.

A queen can live as long as five years and lay up to one million eggs during her lifetime.

WASPS AND BEES,
AND THEIR IMPORTANCE
TO HUMANS

How They Are Useful

- Bees are the most important **pollinators** of flowering plants, including fruits and vegetables.

- Honeybees are farmed for their honey and beeswax.

- Many parasitic wasps help protect crops. Some feed on pest insects that destroy crops. Others lay their eggs in or on pest insects, killing them.

Beehives in a Kiwi Fruit Orchard ▼

Bee Stinging a Human ▲

How They Are Harmful

- Wasps and bees sometimes sting humans. In most cases, they sting when people disturb their nests or do something to upset them.

- Some people are **allergic** to wasp and bee stings. Scientists believe that between one and two million people in the United States alone are severely allergic to the stings of wasps and bees.

GLOSSARY

allergic: Having a strong physical reaction to something that is normally harmless

antennae: Thin, movable parts of an insect's head that help it to sense its surroundings

burrow: A tunnel or hole

host: A plant or animal that benefits a parasite but gets no benefit from the parasite

larva: Immature, early-stage forms of animals

life cycle: The stages, or phases, of an animal's development

mate: To join with another animal in order to produce offspring

paralyze: To make an animal unable to move

parasites: Animals that live on other animals and use them to survive

pollen: A powdery substance created by plants so that they can reproduce

pollinators: Insects that carry pollen from one part of a plant to another, or from one plant to another

prey: Animals that are hunted and eaten by other animals

solitary: Living alone; without company

species: Types of animals that have some physical characteristics in common

swarm: A very large number of insects moving together

tropical: Areas that are very warm throughout the year

INDEX